BookLife PUBLISHING

©2023
BookLife Publishing Ltd.
King's Lynn, Norfolk
PE30 4LS, UK

All rights reserved.
Printed in China.

A catalogue record for this book is available from the British Library.

ISBN: 978-1-80505-025-4

Written by:
Charis Mather
Adapted by:
Noah Leatherland
Edited by:
Rod Barkman
Designed by:
Amy Li

All facts, statistics, web addresses and URLs in this book were verified as valid and accurate at time of writing. No responsibility for any changes to external websites or references can be accepted by either the author or publisher.

AN INTRODUCTION TO BOOKLIFE RAPID READERS...

Packed full of gripping topics and twisted tales, BookLife Rapid Readers are perfect for older children looking to propel their reading up to top speed. With three levels based on our planet's fastest animals, children will be able to find the perfect point from which to accelerate their reading journey. From the spooky to the silly, these roaring reads will turn every child at every reading level into a prolific page-turner!

CHEETAH
The fastest animals on land, cheetahs will be taking their first strides as they race to top speed.

MARLIN
The fastest animals under water, marlins will be blasting through their journey.

FALCON
The fastest animals in the air, falcons will be flying at top speed as they tear through the skies.

Photo Credits – Images are courtesy of Shutterstock.com. With thanks to Getty Images, Thinkstock Photo and iStockphoto. Recurring images – Marina Santiaga, aopsan, MG Drachal, Roxana Bashyrova, backUp. Cover – MagicPics, Seahorse Vector, Redcollegiya. 4–5 – conrado, Marben. 6–7 – Digital Storm. 8–9 – Catmando, Ian Luck. 10–11 – TamaraLSanchez, Chamille White. 12–13 – Anastasija Popova, Callipso88. 14–15 – New Africa, cityfoto24, GRISIK NATALIA, Igor Kovalchuk. 16–17 – Firn, SeraphP. 18–19 – GUDKOV ANDREY, VBakunin68 (Wikimedia Commons). 20–21 – ANN_UDOD, Angelos Vergekios (Wikimedia Commons). 22–23 – CANONGROUP, Warpaint. 24–25 – Daniel Eskridge, steved_np3. 26–27 – ploy2907, dore art. 28–29 – wavebreakmedia, Luis Molinero. 30 – T Studio.

CONTENTS

PAGE 4   The Mystery of the Unicorn
PAGE 6   Unicorn Spotter's Guide
PAGE 8   A Sharp Point
PAGE 10   Pure and a Cure
PAGE 12   Everything We Know
PAGE 14   Food for Thought
PAGE 16   Easy Mistake to Make…
PAGE 20   Impostor!
PAGE 24   Hidden Hideouts
PAGE 26   Written in the Stars
PAGE 28   Creatures of Myth
PAGE 31   Glossary
PAGE 32   Index

Words that look like <u>this</u> are explained in the glossary on page 31.

THE MYSTERY OF THE UNICORN

Have you ever seen a unicorn? Probably not. They are mythical creatures, after all. Mythical creatures appear in stories and <u>legends</u>, but no one knows for sure if they are real.

You might have heard of unicorns and their magical powers. Could they have existed in the past? Could they still exist today? If so, what might they be like?

Some stories about unicorns date back thousands of years. There are even old paintings and drawings of these magical creatures. They give us a pretty good idea what unicorns may look like.

How much is true? How much is make-believe? You will have to decide that yourself.

UNICORN
SPOTTER'S GUIDE

COAT
Clean and white!

Unicorns may look slightly different from one story to the next. Stories from different times and places might disagree on what a unicorn looks like. You can always spot a unicorn by its horn, though.

If you think you may have seen a unicorn, use this guide:

LONG, TWISTED HORN
The horn is the most magical part of a unicorn. All unicorns have one.

BEARDS?
Some drawings show unicorns with beards!

SILKY HAIR
Unicorns have long, flowing tails and <u>manes</u>.

STRONG HORSE BODY
Unicorns look a lot like horses.

A SHARP POINT

A unicorn's horn is very important. Without it, they would just look like normal horses. What do their horns do, exactly?

It would be nice to think that unicorns only use their horns for fun and games. Their horns have a much more serious use in the wild.

There are many animals that use their horns to fight off attackers. It would not be surprising if unicorns did this too, even though they are said to be peaceful.

With a horn as impressive as theirs, animals are sure to think twice before going after a unicorn. Unicorns do not just use their horns for protection, though. They are magical, after all!

PURE
AND A CURE

Unicorns are said to have the power to heal people and make things <u>pure</u>. The stories say they can do this with the touch of their horn.

As well as cuts and bruises, a unicorn's horn is said to also <u>cure</u> sickness and <u>diseases</u>. The tales say their horns can also make <u>poisoned</u> water safe again.

People in the past hoped to use some of this magic. Some people made cups out of what they thought were unicorn horns. They thought they could drink out of them without worrying about poison.

Other people tried to make unicorn horns into a powder and use it for medicine. Perhaps that is why people never seem to see unicorns these days...

EVERYTHING
WE KNOW

Unicorns are thought to live for hundreds of years. They are said to live out in the wild in groups called herds.

Since unicorns mostly keep hidden from people, no one knows how big these herds are. If you ever see a unicorn on its own, keep an eye out for others.

Some newer stories say unicorns come in different colours. In most <u>traditional</u> tales, unicorns have white coats. White is a colour that sometimes shows something is pure and peaceful.

Who knows, though? Maybe there are colourful unicorns out there that we just haven't seen yet.

FOOD FOR THOUGHT

Unicorns probably have a similar diet to horses. They most likely eat plants they find in the wild, such as grass, flowers and berries.

Thanks to their magical powers, unicorns do not have to worry about accidentally eating poisonous plants. That means unicorns can eat pretty much whatever they want!

The more colourful a unicorn's food, the better. As well as flowers and berries, some people say unicorns eat rainbows as a special treat.

We can only imagine what rainbows might taste like. With all those different colours, they probably have lots of different flavours. They must be delicious!

EASY MISTAKE TO MAKE...

Remember, lots of animals have horns, so be careful when trying to find a unicorn. Some animals may look like a unicorn, but they might have more than one horn.

A few different types of deer and antelopes have horns. They might look similar to unicorns, but remember... count the horns!

Some creatures may have one horn, but that does not make them a unicorn.

Do not get tricked by these other animals. They are <u>impostors</u>. Their horns are not even magical!

NARWHALS

Narwhals live in the world's coldest seas. A narwhal horn can grow up to three metres long. However, it is not magical, and it is not really a horn.

A narwhal's horn is actually a tusk. Tusks are more like teeth, but they can still grow out of an animal's head.

RHINOCEROSES

Greater one-horned rhinoceroses have a horn on the end of their noses, not their forehead. Their horns are also a different shape to unicorn horns.

Their horns are much shorter and look like a stump. They are not spiral shaped.

IMPOSTOR!

QILINS

Qilins have a single horn on their head, just like unicorns. However, qilins are much more colourful than unicorns. They also have different bodies.

In old drawings, qilins look like deer covered in <u>scales</u>. Their heads look similar to Asian dragons.

Monoceroses look looks like a few different animals. Stories say they have the head of a deer, the tail of a boar, the body of a horse and feet like an elephant.

They are said to have one very long horn on their heads.

PEGASUS

Unicorns sometimes get mixed up with another mythical creature called Pegasus. However, the legends say that Pegasus is the only one of its kind.

Both Pegasus and unicorns look similar to horses. They both also have pure white coats, which is why people get them confused.

However, Pegasus and unicorns have some big differences. Pegasus has large wings like a bird and can fly.

It does not have any magical powers like a unicorn. Pegasus does not have a horn like a unicorn, either.

HIDDEN HIDEOUTS

Finding a unicorn can be very hard. They like to live in quiet, wooded areas and like to stay away from people. They like peace.

There are stories of some lucky humans who have met unicorns. This only happens when unicorns sense that the person has a pure heart.

To find a unicorn, you would need to find a peaceful spot in the woods. You need to be very quiet if you do not want to scare it off.

If a unicorn is nearby and can sense that you can be trusted, it might come up to you. If you are lucky, it might rest its head in your lap.

WRITTEN IN THE STARS

One place to find a unicorn is in the stars. Stars make patterns called <u>constellations</u>. These patterns are given names based on what their shape looks like.

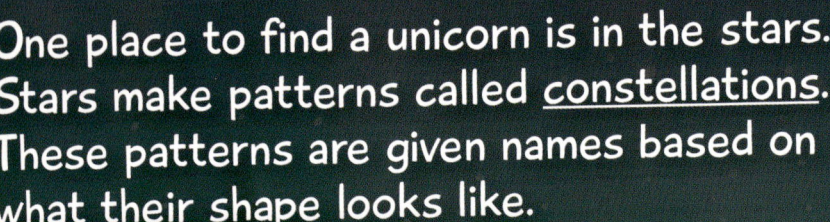

There is a constellation called 'Monoceros' (like that impostor from earlier), but this is just an old Greek word for 'unicorn'. It was discovered by scientists in the 1600s.

The unicorn stars can be seen in the Northern <u>Hemisphere</u> in the winter. However, the sky needs to be very dark and clear for you to see it. The stars are as tricky to spot as an actual unicorn!

The biggest star in the unicorn constellation is 6 times bigger than the Sun and over 1,000 times brighter.

CREATURES OF MYTH

Unicorns are mysterious creatures. That is what makes them so interesting. There is so much we do not know about them.

We may never find the answers to the questions we have. So, we might just have to use our imagination.

The best way to find out more about unicorns is to keep reading about them. There are so many stories to choose from!

Each story might tell you something new about unicorns. Who knows what you will find out?

If we know one thing for sure about unicorns, it is that we do not know much about them. Mythical creatures can always surprise us with new things. There is so much more to discover about them. Will you be the one to do it?

Keep your eyes peeled and maybe you could be the one to find a unicorn!

GLOSSARY

CONSTELLATIONS groups of stars that make a pattern or shape

CURE to heal

DISEASES illnesses that cause harm to someone's health

HEMISPHERE half of the planet

IMPOSTORS things that pretend to be something else

LEGENDS stories from the past that may have a mix of truth and made-up things

MANES long sections of hair that grow on animals' necks

POISONED having been made dangerous or deadly when eaten or drunk

PURE clean or innocent

SCALES small, overlapping flakes, as found on animals such as fish and snakes

TRADITIONAL how things have been done or thought about for a long time

INDEX

HORNS 6–11, 16–21, 23

MONOCEROSES 21, 26

NARWHALS 18

PEGASUS 22–23

POWERS 4, 10, 14, 23

QILINS 20

RAINBOWS 15

RHINOCEROSES 19

STARS 26–27